3—

To Bruce,
with best wishes
for a Happy Birthday
"In the clubs' own
swinging time."
and love from
 Aunt Nell & Uncle Bill

1953.

LOVE THAT GOLF

It CAN Be Better Than You Think

Other Books by Don Herold

SO HUMAN

BIGGER AND BETTER

THERE OUGHT TO BE A LAW

OUR COMPANIONATE GOLDFISH

STRANGE BEDFELLOWS

DOING EUROPE AND VICE VERSA

LOVE THAT GOLF

It CAN Be Better Than You Think

by Don Herold

Illustrated by the Author

A. S. BARNES and COMPANY
New York

DEDICATED TO MY WIFE AND TO
EVERY OTHER WOMAN WHO HAS
HAD TO PUT UP PATIENTLY FOR
YEARS WITHOUT END WITH A MAN
WHO IS A DAMN FOOL ABOUT GOLF

CONTENTS

		Page
	"THAT HAPPY ADVENTURE, GOLF" . .	15

Chapter

1	YOU CAN'T MIX GOLF WITH HATE—OR HASTE	36
2	YOU CAN'T SCORE IF YOU CAN'T PUTT .	40
3	GETTING THOSE APPROACH SHOTS UP FOR ONE PUTT, I HOPE	56
4	DON'T LET THE LONG SHOTS PANIC YOU	69
5	YOU'VE GOTTA TAKE AIM	93
6	LET GOLF PLAY YOU	96
7	"I'M TOO OLD TO LEARN—I'LL NEVER PLAY ANY BETTER"	102
8	DON'T BE SO DAMNED DULL . . .	108
9	GOOD GOLF IS SHAKEN ONLY OUT OF A PRACTICE BAG	116
10	TRAPS AND OTHER TROUBLES . . .	120
11	ALONG ABOUT HERE	134

LOVE THAT GOLF

It CAN Be Better Than You Think

Be as happy as you can, but appear more so.

Mrs. Jack Gardner

The individual and not the event is the creator of happiness. If the event be the creator of happiness, and happiness must wait upon propitious circumstances, very few people can ever be happy.

Raymond Leslie Goldman

Noah to the Lord, in *Green Pastures:* "I ain't very much, but I's all I got."

I played lousy today, but what the hell—I'll play good tomorrow.

Don Herold

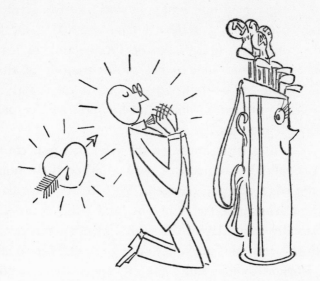

"That Happy Adventure, Golf"

GOLF MAY BE A HUSSY, BUT I LOVE HER.

This love affair has been the thrill of my life.

Golf treats me nasty at times, kicks me in the teeth, and humiliates me in front of my friends, but I go on loving her as if she were clean, decent and divine.

I'm just a mine-run, drug-store golfer, but over the years I have found golf delicious and delightful, and I find it more and more a **source** of pleasure as the years go by.

I've given so much to golf, and golf has given so much to me, that I believe I have a book in me for other "ordinary" golfers, for beginners, and for many folks who would like to get more fun out of their game, while maybe improving it some as they go along.

Golf has been so much fun for me that I've practically planned my life around it.

I built a little house on the edge of a golf course at Brookfield, Connecticut, and another little house on the edge of a golf course at Vero Beach, Florida. I play at least nine holes of golf and practice a little practically every day of the year. I'm not wealthy and I haven't retired. I am lucky enough to be able to take my work with me, and I take it where there is golf, and I even get more work out of myself every day by promising myself some golf when I'm through.

I started golf pretty late in life, yet I have improved my game every year. (That's not so hard to do when you start at nothin'.) I expect to keep on improving it until I'm eighty. As my muscles weaken, I plan to get cagier at the game.

And, what's most important, I've learned how to enjoy golf even when it's bad.

That's love!

A lot of golfers get no better at their golf, and a lot of them get nothing but heartaches out of their game.

To paraphrase Thoreau, many golfers lead lives of quiet desperation.

That is what I want to remedy in this book.

A theatrical acquaintance of mine, Richard Mayers, the producer, told me that he had quit golf "because it is an unhappy game."

There are many golf players who get mad at golf almost every time they play. They are in a constant lovers' quarrel with the game. Either that, or they just whack around, not even scratching the surface of the pleasure to be had from it.

I, too, suffered at golf for several years, until I adopted the attitude that I want to recommend to you in this book.

There was a time when I thought there should be a sign over the gate of every golf clubhouse: *"Where every prospect pleases, and only golf is vile."* But now I respond to Chick Evans' line: "When I was a kid coming into *that happy adventure, golf.* . . ."

I began to enjoy golf when I decided that though I might never be a consistently low-score golfer, and though I would often play poorly, I could devote my life to studying and learning the game, and would surely and gradually improve it . . . to some extent, at least.

I think Richard Mayers gave up golf and took to

tennis too easily. I think a lot of golfers get mad at golf too readily.

You don't give up married life (not always) because it isn't continuously blissful. Unless it is fundamentally a bad match, you make up after every fallin' out. And it grows better as you grow older.

I hope I can help you to have fewer fallin' outs with your golf.

I know that anybody's golf can be stinking at times. Mine is especially variable because I have an up-and-down nervous system, and an undependable supply of energy. I get tireder sooner than the sturdy young peasants with whom I sometimes play or the sturdy old bucks with whom I more often play. They were raised on farms; I was raised in a hot house; hell, I was 45 years old before I knew it was any fun to get up out of a chair.

Those older golfers usually have horrible looking swings, yet many of them get excellent scores. (I'd rather play pretty and score worse!)

I'm the kind of golfer who shoots a 73 looking in a sporting goods store window or coming out on the Friday evening train. You might say I'm a golf dreamer.

The biggest kick I get out of golf is in thinking of myself as an humble, lifelong student of the game. I get my kick out of trying to learn more about it,

I regret that
I have but
one life
to give
to golf

studying it, practicing it, taking lessons, talking it, experimenting, reading books about it, trying, hoping, praying . . . and, incidentally, playing it.

Every time I start a game I remember Emerson's remark that when he left home on a journey he "set aside a certain amount of money to be robbed of." I anticipate a certain number of unhappy strokes. Walter Hagen used to say that he expected four or five bad shots in every game.

"Permit yourself a certain degree of failure in advance," said Ernest Dichter, Ph.D. He wasn't speaking of golf, but it applies.

If I have a bad day, I've merely slipped back a few feet on my theoretical uphill climb. Mountain climbers don't go home every time they lose a yard.

I'll never give up the idea that I'm gaining on it.

The thing we golfers forget is that golf is a damned difficult game (until we learn to play it easily).

Learning golf is a whole lot more like learning to play the violin than learning how to pitch horseshoes or play hopscotch.

Golf is profound—believe it or not, you golf scorners and scoffers.

We would never expect to play a violin like Heifetz or Kreisler after 10 lessons.

It may take me (and you) the rest of our lives to

learn to play good golf. Well, that's all right. It's nice work, isn't it?

Al Collins said at Sleepy Hollow one day: "Not one in 1,000 novices ever looks like a real golfer in less than three years."

We keep comparing ourselves with the pros, and we forget that the pros started as caddies when they were 12 years old, and that they have 7 or 8 hours a day of playing and practicing, whereas the majority of us after-work or week-end golfers play, at most, 6 or 8 hours a week, with no practice, and maybe we never touch a stick all winter—who do we think we are!

Our ignominy is constantly increased by the ever-lasting comparison we are forced to make with the pros. We get par and sub-par thrown at us in the tournament reports in the newspapers every day of the year. They even print par on the score cards. (There ought to be another score card for us, the first five years we play.) We are amateurs trying to play a professional game. However, it's so much fun, that if we have any sense, we won't let it break our hearts.

Furthermore, the golf courses are laid out for professionals—not for us. The golf courses are built for about 3% of the players. Yet we dubs, sub-dubs and fair-to-middlers pay 97% of the cost of supporting the courses.

In recent years $100,000 has been spent on one golf course I know—that at the Ponte Vedra Inn at Ponte Vedra Beach in Florida—to improve and *simplify* it under the direction of golf architect Robert Trent Jones. They have removed 100 traps, widened some of the fairways, installed optional "average" tees, and otherwise "humanized" the course, without spoiling it for the champions. This kind of sense will in time be lavished on other golf courses.

I can draw better cartoons and I can write a darned sight better than Hogan, Snead, Demaret and all the others, yet I'm supposed to feel peewee because I shoot only fair golf.

"Golf isn't your business; it's your hobby," says Johnny Farrell.

Part of the glorious torture of golf is that you not only have to learn it; you have to relearn it all over again and again. It's wonderful agony, and you might as well relax and enjoy same.

Then comes a good shot and, with it, the aesthetic kick that only a good golf shot can give you. I actually believe there's no greater thrill in life than a golf shot authentically smacked.

Silly, isn't it?

But isn't it the essence of every hobby that it is

They laughed
when I sat down
to tee off

utterly inane, insane and un-utilitarian? You have the devotee's joy of dedicating yourself to a dream, to a lost cause, to a purpose which you and you alone prize. Isn't that the thrill of any love affair? You throw yourself overboard for something in which nobody else begins to see the heavenly virtues which appeal to you.

And this may explain our intolerance of the other fellow's hobby, whatever it may be—an intolerance usually much more vehement than religious, racial or national intolerance. I have a yachtsman friend, for example, who would like to kill me when I start to talk golf. And vice versa.

Walter J. Travis said that golf is more than a mere game; it is a religion.

Speaking of re-learning the game, I notice that even the pros have to do that. The best of them still spend hours at practice.

Paderewski used to say that he always practiced three hours a day; if he missed one hour, he, himself, noticed it; if he missed two hours, the critics noticed it; if he missed three hours, the public noticed it.

I've taken hundreds of golf lessons and I practice more than most players. I'd just as soon take a lesson or practice as play.

I believe in taking lessons, and I like pros. They are, on the whole, about the finest group of men I know. There's something about teaching this game that produces gentlemen.

Once in a while I shoot a good game of golf, and I'd never do it if it weren't for the pros. When I hit a ball well, I owe every inch of the swing to one golf pro or another.

When I hit a ball lousily, I owe it to me.

If I were starting golf all over, I'd take lessons for a year before playing a round.

One reason that we need pros is to act as mirrors. We fall into faults of which we are unaware, unless someone tells us.

There's just one thing I'd like to ask pros: couldn't golf be taught to music? It is essentially a game of rhythm, and I think somebody ought to set it to music. I'm sure I could swing better if accompanied by a good swing band.

One thing a golf pro can do, too, is to help you swing pretty. And I think that good looking form is one of the secrets of good golf. Look beautiful and you'll play beautiful.

However, some old codgers with whom I play, play mighty ugly and beat the pants off of me.

But the rule is, look funny and you'll play funny.

Incidentally, I think a good pro is one who can tell you *one* thing which will cover six points or correct

Golf should be taught to music

six faults. I've had pros who have told me too many things at one time. We poor dumb pupils can't possibly comprehend more than two or three new ideas in one lesson.

(One smart old pro told me that he frequently advised his "old banker" pupils to go home and throw rocks at a tin can in their back yards.)

Read the golf books. There are a couple of dozen of them that you should have in your library. You might as well go completely nuts while you're at it.

But after you've taken the lessons and after you've read the books, you're on your own. A man's golf is, ultimately, between himself and his God.

I've kept notes on every lesson I've ever taken, and, as I write, I'll crib from them and from some of the books I've read.

One thing that will help you keep calm while playing golf is to remember that nobody gives a darn about your bad golf but you.

You don't need to be self-conscious about your poor golf. It isn't a disgrace to hit a bad shot or a series of bad shots. Nobody is damning or condemning you. Each of us is interested only in his own golf—not the other fellow's. Remember *that*, when you dub a shot.

If you dub enough of them, quit playing and take lessons and practice, or both.

But your bad days at golf are not at all serious to your fellow players. If anything, each of *your* bad shots builds the other fellow's ego.

Don't apologize, and don't tell how good you were last Saturday. Just let your day's bad golf slide. Take it in your stride. You can't alibi a 100 score down to 80.

I liked a remark made by a man with whom I had been playing golf for the first time. As we finished, he said: "No matter how I talk about my golf, *that* is the way I play."

Another day in Florida, I was asked to play golf with a young advertising writer from Chicago. He played terribly, but he was completely genial about it. No apologies or alibis. He didn't share his pain with the rest of us, if he had any. Several months later, the head of a big advertising agency in Chicago wrote me that he was thinking of hiring this young man and asked me what I knew about him. I answered that I knew very little about the fellow, but that he played bad golf more pleasantly than anybody else I'd ever seen, and I'd bet he would be a good man in any organization. This was sufficient recommendation, and today the young man is one of the top executives in the agency.

Golf is life. If you can't take golf, you can't take life.

There are days, it's true, when golf seems like a bad dose of medicine, and all you can do is to take it.

One way to enjoy your golf more, when you are starting, is not to think of your score, but to regard the game as a fishing expedition. When you go out for a game, just see how many good hits you can catch.

Learn how to be somewhat lazy at your golf. "I believe the lazier you tend to be, the longer you will live," says Dr. Peter J. Steincrohn in his book *How to Stop Killing Yourself* (Wilfred Funk, Inc., New York). (And the longer you live, the more golf you'll get to play, say I.) "Remember, the lazy tortoise lives out his 200 to 300 year span, and the leisurely, unhurried elephant exists from 150 to 200 years. Will power is the ability to play *nine* holes of golf. It takes will power to stop short of extreme fatigue."

Speaking of elephants, Bobby Jones, himself, says that one of his friends told him the best golf lesson he ever had was watching an old elephant in a zoo, swaying easily and lazily from side to side.

Perhaps the greatest apostle of serene relaxation in America today is singer Bing Crosby. Relaxation is 90 percent of his charm. And Bing no doubt learned a lot about relaxation on the golf course, or maybe he's such a good golfer because he was born relaxed. "My relaxation in golf is one of the smartest invest-

The first thing
you have to learn
is how to tell a
No. 6 iron from
a No. 9 iron
upside down

ments I ever made," says Bing. "The way I look at it, every fellow is, in a way, a factory. If he doesn't keep his machinery in good shape he'll go into the red. As a kid caddy, the first thing I learned was that tension is ruinous to a golf swing. And I've seen enough in business to be impressed by the danger of tight, strained nerves to the men who pound themselves at their jobs. That's a risk I am not going to take."

There's poetry in this game, and in men who play it well. Watching Paul Runyan hit a spoon shot one day, Horton Smith said, "Watch Paul's unhurried swing. It's as lazy as a Spanish siesta, as delicately fashioned as a flower petal."

One thing you must realize about improving your golf is that you will come to plateaus when you will show no progress, and may even show retrogression. But if you are studying the game, you will come out eventually on a higher level.

Personally, I find that strange things affect my scores. For example, coffee. I'm allergic to it, and I ran my 9-hole score up 15 points one day, believe it or not, by drinking two cups of coffee for breakfast that morning. I was too excited.

But, shucks, Grantland Rice says he saw Craig Wood shoot an 88 in one tournament round and a 67 the next day. And he saw Bobby Jones shoot a 79 in one Masters' at Atlanta, and a 63 in a friendly round a few days later.

If you are going to take golf too seriously, it will make an old man or old woman of you, when it is supposed to make you young. It isn't the game; it's your bad mental reactions that can give you real fatigue. A missed 18 inch putt can be more exhausting than a well-hit 225 yard drive and the walk to the ball.

If you play, play.

Karl A. Menninger, in his book *Love Against Hate,* says: "People who don't play are potentially dangerous. There seems to be a general idea that recreation is all right if one doesn't take it too seriously. My belief is that much greater danger lies in not taking it seriously enough."

The drift of my book, then, is paradoxical. I suggest that you be more serious about your golf, and thus quit taking it so seriously.

My real purpose in writing this book is to help you get more fun out of learning how to enjoy an "unhappy game."

But something I'll say may take five strokes from your score.

If I add five strokes to your score, sue me!

I'll say you've gotta learn to enjoy bad golf; that's the only kind there is

CHAPTER 1

You Can't Mix Golf with Hate —or Haste

YOU CAN'T PLAY GOOD GOLF WHEN YOU ARE MAD AT your wife.

You can't play good golf when you are mad at golf.

You can't play good golf when you are mad at anything or anybody—the weather, your business, your golfing partners, the stock market, the foursome ahead of you, the foursome behind you.

If your wife interferes with your golf, get a new wife. If your business interferes with your golf, get a new business.

You've got to be at peace with the universe when you play this game. That's a big order. But golf is a big order. It's worth it.

Maybe golf is the best reason you've ever had to try to calm down.

You can't play good golf if you eat a sandwich on the run and barely catch a train and arrive at the course in a nervous sweat. I've never yet seen anybody arrive at the first tee in a stew and play a good game. The chances are he bloops the first hole, and shoots badly all day.

Johnny Farrell tells of his experience with Walter Hagen, one day, when they were scheduled for an important match, and Hagen was late. Walter explained that he had been shaving.

Johnny cracked that he must have had a month-old beard.

Hagen then explained that when he had a match to play he began to relax as soon as he woke up. "Everything I do, I do slow and easy." That went for stroking the razor, getting dressed and eating his breakfast. "I'm practically in slow motion. By the time I tee off, I'm so used to taking my time that it's impossible to hurry my swing."

This is from Johnny's book, *If I Were in Your*

Golf Shoes (Henry Holt and Company, New York)— a book you should have in your golf library.

If I seem inclined to quote from the old-timers more than from the new crop of outstanding golfers, it is because they were, on the whole, somewhat more articulate. They were golfing pioneers, and they had to formulate golfing philosophies. Furthermore, they grew old in golf and had more time to think about it —to ripen in golf, as it were.

You, too, can learn to approach golf in less of a fuss. Do various things to build up relaxation. Take some easy practice swings. Waggle. Feel the club head. Feel out your arm and leg relaxation. Feel out your follow through.

Start for your golf date ahead of time. Get there in plenty of time to let your blood pressure stop climbing.

Hagen says we should saunter up to our golf "gracefully," with both body and mind as if we were departing upon an evening's stroll. "Approach each shot carefully but casually. Hit and run golf never got anybody to first base. Hurry has no part in the sport. It is a game of leisure."

He says further that we should not make instant decisions, but take time to study each shot, each situation.

Most of us know the penalty of hurrying swings, yet we keep on hurrying them. Nearly all the 90 shooters put costly haste into the top 10 inches of their swing. The 100 shooters hurry all the way up and all the way down. They uncock their wrists at the top and hit with stiff arms.

Wiffy Cox says that only the champions "can hit a golf ball slow enough."

Half our bad shots are caused by our hurry to look up and see what we've done. Golf is not a good spectator sport from the player's standpoint. It has been said that nobody ever looked up and saw a good shot.

Perhaps one reason that so many of us find golf such wonderful medicine is that we know that in order to play it at all well, we can't mix it with hate or haste.

There's something spiritual about this damned game, after all.

Putting doesn't interest me

CHAPTER 2

You Can't Score if You Can't Putt

THIS BOOK IS WRITTEN BASS-ACKWARDS. MOST GOLF
BOOKS OPEN WITH CHAPTERS ON THE DRIVE, AND GRADU-
ALLY WORK DOWN TO A SKIMPY PAGE OR TWO ON PUTT-
ING, AT THE END, AS IF PUTTING WERE MERELY A
STEPCHILD OF GOLF. IN MY MIND, PUTTING IS THE BASIS
OF GOLF. IF I WERE A PRO, I'D START EVERY NEW PUPIL
OFF ON PUTTING, BECAUSE I BELIEVE PUTTING CONTAINS
THE ELEMENTS OF EVERY OTHER GOLF STROKE. A DRIVE
IS MERELY AN ELONGATED PUTT.

As I came in from a game one day, a wise old golfing friend of mine said, "How was your putting?" He didn't even bother to ask about my score.

"Not too good."

"You can't score if you can't putt."

Fortunately, anybody can learn to putt.

Claude Harmon says, "A good putter can be made."

But few of us take the trouble to make one out of ourselves.

Few of us realize how much poor putting has to do with poor scores. I never really realized it until I started playing with a friend who liked to place small bets on our putts, and we kept a careful record of them.

Every time I got a good total score, I found I was sinking several one-putts.

You can't score well even if your greens are all two-putt greens.

Keep a record of your putts up in the corner of the little score square. Don't write down the 2's—just the 1's, 3's, etc. Then you'll really know how well you're putting. Small bets on putts will help improve your score.

Approaching and putting are the only hope of us latecomers to golf—of us guys with thin wrists and no especial athletic ability—of us guys with inborn clodhopper co-ordination. We can never learn to out-slug the fellows who took up golf in their boyhood and who are physically organized, and maybe still years younger than we. You know, those guys who ought to be driving a truck in the first place.

But we can out-practice them and perhaps develop a better game than theirs, around the greens.

Fortunately, you can be pretty wild all over the course and still arrive with a fairly good score for the hole if you can shoot with surety from 75 to 100 yards on in.

Walter Hagen missed twelve fairways in one Eastern Open, yet scored a 65 for the round.

One reason we may neglect putting is that we may think it is sissy. Well, so what! It's fair to win by fair means or by putting well, isn't it?

I've seen good, he-guy long hitters play beautifully up to the neighborhood of the greens and then throw their scores away by messing up approach shots and putts. They don't regard the short game as golf!

The teaching pros don't pay enough attention to our putting. They are apt to say almost nothing about it unless we press them. But some of the best pro help I've had has been from Mike Kundrat at the Candlewood Lake Club at Brookfield, Conn., on putting. Take a lesson *on putting* from your pro every so often.

Practice putting a little bit every day before you play. You can lose your putting touch overnight, and one or two dozen putts before you start will do wonders for your score. Keep practicing until you feel yourself stroking them in again.

Gene Sarazen says that most of us make the mistake of starting to practice the long putts first. He advises us to start with the short ones and gradually work back. I've found that a good putting exercise is to putt from 12 to 18 inches from the hole and actually sweep the ball into the hole, letting the putter pass over the hole.

Be sure you have a putter that is a natural for you. One winter when I couldn't get to Florida, I bought five types of putters and practiced with them on the living room rug all winter, keeping a careful score on each type, and I finally found the one I liked best. Sammy Snead tried out 18 putters in one year when he was trying to find his way to better putting. My wife says she's going to meet her doom by rolling out from under herself on a golf ball on the living room rug some night.

When you step up to a putt, remember that you've got to concentrate like a setting hen. Everything else in the world must be put out of your mind.

"That earthquake didn't seem to bother you."

DEATH ON
THE LIVING ROOM RUG

"What earthquake?"

You've got to want passionately to sink that putt. You've got to mean to sink it. You're just going to sink it—that's all there is to it.

Don't let anybody or anything hurry you or disturb you.

I believe the first rule for good putting is to take time enough to get settled, compose yourself, make peace with your God and the world, let the universe quit whirling, get the line right, get your grip right, rehearse, relax and shoot right. Don't putt muddled.

You absolutely have to take enough time to see every inch of what your putter is doing on the back stroke and on the follow through. You have to see it lined up at right angles to the line of flight, and you have to see it go slowly straight back and slowly straight out the line to the hole. Take time, time, time, time.

You can't snip at a putt and get anywhere.

There is almost a slight stop or pause at the "top" of your backswing in putting, as there is in every other good golf shot. Dick Chapman once said that he counts to himself on putts and on every other shot, "one-PAUSE-hit."

Bobby Jones in his autobiography, *Down the Fairway* (Blue Ribbon Books, Garden City, N. Y.) says

45

There is such a thing
as being too much of
an individualist
at putting

that he early resolved never to putt until he took time "to get my breathing and heart tranquilized."

Babe Didrikson Zaharias, in her book *Championship Golf* (A. S. Barnes, New York) relates an old saying on the greens: "Miss 'em quick."

I like to crouch a little, in order to get down to business. You've gotta mean business when you putt.

Sorta stand with your right shoulder in under and your left shoulder up, so that you'll be in a position to go out smoothly in a line to the hole. Relax your right leg to make it additionally easy for you to go out to the hole.

Keeping your weight mostly on your left foot helps prevent sway.

I let my right arm rest and slide on my right leg. The arm must leave the leg slightly on the longer putts.

I use a reverse overlap grip, with both thumbs straight down the center of the top of the shaft, with both hands as a unit, facing each other, palms opposing. The reverse overlap grip gives you more control by putting all four fingers of your right hand on the club.

If I find that my putts are going to the right, I usually discover my right hand has slipped down underneath.

Gene Sarazen, a good putter, says he gets more

control of his putter by extending his right forefinger down the shaft of the club. I'd putt with one finger in my ear if it would help my putting.

The club head has to be kept low, close to the ground, on the backswing and on the follow through.

The most important thing of all is to *go out with the ball* with your putter—out for 6 or 7 inches, at least. That's what I watch—that line on which my putter is to travel—the line I have decided is right.

This line may not always be straight to the hole. It may go 6 inches to the south or north, depending on the slope. But it starts out straight. As far as you are concerned, it is a straight line. All putts are, in essence, only 6-inch putts. I keep my toes parallel to this line, wherever it goes.

I try to think of my putter as being glued to the ball for 6 or 7 inches.

Somebody else put it well: Imagine yourself driving a 6 inch spike right through the center of the ball.

If you don't go out with the ball, the ball won't have the oomph necessary to carry it straight to the hole.

You've got to keep your noggin still until you hear the ball drop in the cup.

The angle of your club face must at all times be at a perfect right angle to the intended line of travel.

Before you putt, study the situation. Maybe you should squat down to get the real slope. "Read the green." "Case the green."

Walk up to your putt from several yards behind your ball.

I point my left elbow toward the hole, to help get and keep direction. I like to "feel some air" under my left arm.

The hardest thing for me to do is to keep from pinching my putts in so that they go to the left of the hole. The best cure for this, I've found, is to have my right side sorta collapsed, and to feel about one half inch give in my right hip as I hit the ball. This lets my stroke go through without a yank in.

("You are inclined to pinch your whole game," said Gene Moser, pro at the Royal Park Golf Club at Vero Beach, Florida, to me one day, and he gave a very comic, exaggerated imitation of a man hugging a golf club in close to his body, almost like a poker player playing them close to his chest.)

I like a heavy putter. I like to feel the metal do the work. I believe the weight helps the blade to go through, down the line.

The ball has to be hit firmly from any distance. A putt that is babied will roll all over the lot with every slope and irregularity of the green.

The most help I ever got on my putting was from the wonderful book by Mark G. Harris, *New Angles on Putting and Chip Shots* (Reilly and Lee, Chicago). This was published in 1940 at $1. If you can find a copy now at any price, it will be the best money you ever invested in golf.

Mark Harris (see a later chapter for my rave on this amazing guy) was an engineer, so he tried to reduce putting to its simplest terms.

He reasoned that the first thing to do is to establish the path on which you want the ball to go and line up everything with that line or at right angles to that line.

The fronts of both his toes are parallel to the line of his putt. His feet are straight, at exact right angles to the line of the putt. There's a picture of a "T" square on the cover of his book, which gives you the idea.

He says nine putters out of ten stand with an open stance, and put their putts to the left.

He gets the putter face at a right angle to the line, and keeps it that way through the stroke.

The eyes and head are kept in the same position until the stroke is finished.

He advocates a lot of indoor practice on the rug, and says a player can learn to groove the stroke by swinging a putter along a carpet seam without a ball.

Basing my thinking on the Mark Harris formula, I have worked out a little "bombsight" for putting, as follows:

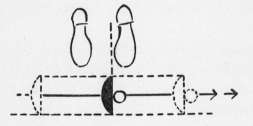

Everything is at right angles to everything in this set-up. The feet and the club face are square to the line of flight, and the club face stays that way.

You can return to this pattern. But if your stance is open or cockeyed or askew, how are you going to know it is the same today as it was yesterday? This "T" square stance is the nearest thing you can have to an aluminum mold or wooden pattern into which you can step for putting.

If you find your vision is chronically such as to make you shoot to the left or right of the hole, aim a fraction of an inch to the right or left by moving your right foot backward or forward very slightly.

A slight inward curve on the backswing is unavoidable on your longer putts.

For longer putts, stand farther away from the ball.

The length of your putt—that is, the length of your forward stroke—is determined by the length of your backstroke.

For longer putts, don't take a short backswing and try to make up for it by a quick, hard hit.

All the time, strive for a graceful, flowing stroke out to the hole.

Roll the ball like a silver dollar. This means you have to stroke slightly up on it, to give it overspin. Overspin keeps the ball rolling close to the ground (not galloping) and tumbles the ball over the brink into the hole.

When you get up to within three feet of the pin, or closer, you have to put more snap into your putts, or you'll soften on them and they'll wander off line. When you get close, you can give them more of a tap.

The Babe says, "I hit short putts and stroke the long ones."

Always see that your putter is resting with its sole flat on the ground—that neither the toe nor the heel is up—that the blade is not tilted forward or backward.

Study the green

There is a "sweet spot" on every putter, from which the ball will take off most soundly and truly. On my putter, this spot is a little inside the center line. My putter, incidentally, has a line on the top of the clubhead, and I think this helps me get better direction.

Don't lift the club up abruptly on the backstroke.

Mark Harris says the control is in the first three fingers of the right hand.

He and other authorities say the left wrist should be firm enough to keep the club head from turning— almost stiff. There is not too much hinge in the wrist at impact. Most golf writers say that the wrists break on the backswing, but not on the forward stroke.

Bobby Locke says lock the left wrist at impact.

Claude Harmon and others are for hitting the ball like the pendulum on a grandfather clock—the pendulum stroke versus the wrist stroke. You keep the head still and putt with stiff arms and stiff rolling shoulders. This doesn't sound too good, but I'm going to investigate it.

I don't completely buy the "never up, never in" theory on putting. I'd rather have my putts die in or near the hole. The ball then has four ways to fall into the hole, not just the front door.

How many putts should you sink, from various

distances? William B. Langford, a well-known builder of golf courses, has made a study of what the average championship putting should be per hole. Here's how he stacks it up:

1 to 3 feet	9 out of 10 putts
3 to 5 feet	8 out of 10 putts
5 to 7 feet	7 out of 10 putts
7 to 9 feet	6 out of 10 putts
9 to 11 feet	5 out of 10 putts
11 to 13 feet	4 out of 10 putts
13 to 15 feet	3 out of 10 putts
15 to 17 feet	2 out of 10 putts
17 to 24 feet	1 out of 10 putts

I'm just as proud to come in with several one-putts on my score card, as I am to come in with a good score.

Edna Ferber once said that many people want to be writers, but few of them want to write. Ben Hogan, speaking of a golfer who wanted to improve his game by some miracle, made this remark: "If this man is really on the level about wanting to improve his golf, he can do what I've done for several years: take a putter and use it from 15 minutes to a couple of hours almost every night, putting at a glass laid on the carpet . . . then he'll begin to get fun out of really studying his golf."

Nice finish for a chip shot — arms outstretched towards the hole

CHAPTER 3

Getting Those Approach Shots Up for One Putt, I Hope

ONE THING I LIKE ABOUT GOLF IS THAT IT IS A GAME in which a little guy like Ben Hogan, after getting himself smashed up into 47 pieces, can come back and lick the tar out of a lot of golfing Tarzans twice his size.

In putting and approaching, especially, we feebles have a chance to catch up with the athletes. Feeling and thinking and practice can make up for physique and muscular power.

Putting and chip shots are 75% of this game.

As you come up to an approach shot, figure where

you want the ball to land. Don't merely wham it generally in the direction of the pin. Study the roll of the green. Maybe you want the ball to land 20 feet this side of the pin and 10 feet to the right.

I used to be way over on all of my short approach shots. But one day I played with an exceptionally good player and I noticed he was landing his shots barely on the green (compared with mine) and letting them roll up to the pin. Since then I've tried to learn how to be "gentle around the greens."

Ben Hogan in his good book, *Power Golf* (A. S. Barnes, New York), says: "When chipping, I try to place the ball where I will get an uphill putt. I don't want a downhill putt, if I can help it, because I am apt to have another putt of about the same distance coming back. So I check the green carefully before making a chip shot."

Study the line, and figure that the face of your club has to move in such a way as to carry the ball on that line. There are two vertical marks on most approach irons, and you should aim them at the point on which you want the ball to land:

AIM THOSE
CLUB HEAD LINES
AT HOLE

I like a pretty square stance for approaching, because the line of my shoulders and the line of my feet help me to take aim, just as in the Mark Harris method of putting. But most teachers say to open the stance; I suppose it's to be sure the left shoulder and hip are out of the way. (In cut shots, the open stance helps you to slash in under the ball from outside in, to impart back-spin, but that's another story.)

Your feet should be fairly close together, so that your hit can be firm and authentic.

Approach shots are crisp, unless you are going to lob 'em, but that, too, will be another story, later.

So you should have a firm feel in the left arm and shoulder and a firm hold on the club with the three small fingers of your left hand, and with the thumb and forefinger of your right hand.

Patty Berg in her excellent book, *Golf* (A. S. Barnes, New York) says: "In playing chip shots from the edge of or a few yards away from the green, I am of the opinion that the firm left hand, wrist, and forearm is the controlling factor. Any collapse of the left wrist is ruinous. I have the feeling that my left wrist remains fairly rigid in drawing the club head through the ball." Patty advocates a shorter grip on the club for these shots.

The right hand should not be under, or it will

The worst thing you
can do is to lift
 the club head up
abruptly from the ball

lock your backswing. I like, in both putts and approach shots, to feel the fat of my right thumb pressing on top of my left thumb.

The distance you get is determined, first, of course, by the club you use, then by the length of your backswing and the power you put into your swing. My No. 8 iron is my pet club, and I use it for almost every shot from 75 yards in, until I get up to within a few feet of the green. (Over traps and bunkers I may slap them or lob them with a heavy No. 11 that I have.)

You should hit iron shots with a blow that descends upon the ball from above, passes underneath it, and takes a divot (or at least cuts the grass) just in front of the point where the ball lay. A swing going straight back helps you achieve this descending hit. And don't get the ball too far forward if this is what you have in mind.

Take a couple of practice swings to make sure that you have the nuts and bolts in your shoulders, arms and hands properly adjusted, and to rehearse the "power" of your swing.

Then start your backswing slowly *along the ground*. The worst thing you can do is to lift the club head up abruptly from the ball with your wrists. Loosen your knees so there will be some yield in your

Take the club head
back as close to
the ground as
possible

body to go back with your swing and out with your swing. Some knee action is absolutely necessary, but it is of course limited. You have to think of a line a couple of feet behind your ball and several feet beyond it, and stick to that line, both ways. Your left arm must be firm, but your body must be as relaxed as if you were pitching horseshoes.

Hold a brief moment at the top of your backswing, as if to think the situation over, to get your poise, and to determine what you are going to do.

James Baird, one of the good old-timers, said: "Generally speaking, iron shots, particularly those with the shorter irons, are played too quickly, and there is too much hurry at the turning point of the stroke."

Look at the bottom of the back of your ball, which is where you want to hit.

Then be crisp and decided about your shot, but relaxed—a big order, I know.

Actually see the club hit the ball and take the divot if any, and go out with the ball several inches. It is important to be watching this process.

don't try to "scoop" the ball up

You mustn't try to scoop the ball, but must depend on the slant of the club face to lift the ball. Remember you hit down into the ball and take a divot or cut the grass after you hit the ball.

Keep your head as steady as a nail on a post until after you have hit the ball. Old Tom Morris said: "Look for a sixpence where the ball was." That may be too long.

Let your left side turn out of the way so the club can bite the ball without any interference from your body.

Swing under with your right shoulder, somewhat as if you were bowling, and straight out to the flag and stay out there pretty like a statue in the park. (Of course, if it's a long swing, your club head itself draws you around eventually.)

Don't under any circumstances stop at the ball. Swing through, sweet chariot. And let your club head stay close to the ground on the follow through, too.

If your ball goes repeatedly to the *left*, it's because you aren't relaxing your right knee and letting your right shoulder roll under and out, or because you are locking your head down so your arms have to go around to the left instead of out with the ball, or because your ball is teed too far forward, or because your grip is turned too far to the right (too far under), or because you are turning your right hand over to the left as you hit.

If you persistently go too far to the *right,* it's because your ball is teed too far back, or you are hitting the ball with a push (hands ahead of the club head) and really sort of shanking it over there.

Sometimes you can straighten out your approach shots by standing closer to the ball. This may cure your pulling in on them.

If you piddle up, it's because you aren't firm enough and are stopping at the ball.

If you have to float over a trap or bunker, and haven't much green to roll on, but must put brakes on your ball, you use a different sort of shot—a sort of lazy pitch or lob. Try a wedge, or an 11 iron, and open your stance and lay back your club face, with the ball placed forward in line with your left toe, and sorta slap clear under through it with fairly loose wrists. This shot is one of the few shots in golf that is hit with a blow that comes down from the outside in. With some practice you can learn how to get backspin with this type of shot.

If I have to go up a hill to a green or over a tree, I use an 8 or 11 iron, play the ball off my front foot, lay the club face back, and give it a long, easy "underhand" swing. If it's up a hill, I follow the slope of the

If you have to
play <u>over</u> a tree
or a <u>barn</u>, put
the ball up forward,
so you will catch
it on the upswing

If you have to play
<u>under</u> a tree, play it
off the right foot, so
you won't catch it on
the upswing, and play
it with a flat swing

ground on my backswing and on my follow through.

When you get up to within 6 or 8 feet of the green, use a slightly lofted iron and play it like a putt. Some players like a 3 iron, some a 4, 5 or 6. I use a No. 7 and I come into it with stiff wrists, but gently.

A lot of my older friends who score well practically putt from 75 yards in if the fairway is smooth, using a 5 or 6 iron almost like a putter. I prefer to trust my No. 8. It's more professional! (I often score badly for my ambitious audacity.) My wife, who plays golf just as she cooks (by the grace of God) with a pinch of this and a pinch of that, usually uses a jigger from 75 feet in and often achieves miracles. Her cooking is better than her golf. I don't even own a jigger. Too many clubs to carry.

Gene Sarazen loves a jigger, he states in his *Thirty Years of Championship Golf* (Prentice-Hall, New York). (This is a most entertaining story of a life of golf.) He says he hit his first golf shot with a jigger and has been partial to it ever since. He can even play over trees with the darned thing.

Mark Harris advocated running up, and playing the shot exactly as if it were a long putt, usually with a 4 iron.

Mike Weiss in his book, *100 Handy Hints on How To Break 100* (Prentice-Hall, New York) says, "If you want to cut down your score, use the run-up or pitch-and-run—not the high-flung pitch shot." Such shots are played with the ball back off the right foot.

As you take your backswing, be sure you keep your left hand underneath. Don't turn it back (don't pronate it) so the back of your left hand is flat, facing the sky.

On wet ground, play the ball back far enough to be sure of hitting the ball before you hit the ground. Otherwise you'll take a scoop of mud before you hit the ball, and get no distance.

On a couple of fairways which often stay moist, on our course in Florida, I run the ball up instead of trying to loft it.

In approach shots always feel that your club head is doing the work. That's one reason for that pause at the top of the backswing. It helps you to feel the weight of the club head and to get set to fling it.

Our pro at Candlewood, Mike Kundrat, almost looks as if he were lashing the ball with a whip. However, don't let this lead you into scooping the ball. Your left arm should stay straight.

And don't get to flipping your pitch shots. If you want your shots to have some backspin and quit chasing across the greens with overspin, you must keep your hands working together and hit the ball firmly.

Many good players address their short shots with the hands slightly ahead of the ball. That is, their club shafts lean slightly to the left. This helps to impart a crisp bite into the ball, and to achieve backspin.

If you are approaching a green that slopes down from you, with a pitch-and-run shot, use a more lofted club than you would on a green that slopes up from you—say a 7 or 8 on the downhill slope and a 3 or 4 on the uphill slope.

As in all other departments, I have to fight my tendency to pinch my arms in on my short shots. I must have a touch of some kind of astringent in my blood.

Willie MacFarlane once said that the best description of a good chip shot is: "the shot before a conceded putt."

go out
wide

on each
side

CHAPTER 4

Don't Let the Long Shots Panic You

WHEN I PLAY A GOOD LONG SHOT, I PLAY IT SOME-
thing like this:

I'm calm when I walk up to the ball. I'm not mad
at man or beast. I'm not scared of the shot just because
it's supposed to be long.

I'm rehearsing in my mind the few things I know
L have to do to hit a good shot. But I'm rehearsing
them as feelings, not as a list of 1, 2, 3's that I have to
check off.

69

I'm remembering that my swing has to be wide and slow (but not *too* slow) and steady and easy. If 35 people are watching, the hell with them.

I'm trying to feel relaxed. One day I watched my daughter on the tee and she was sorta rippling her arms. When I asked her what she was doing, she said, "I'm letting the plasma out." What she meant was that she was letting the tension out. It didn't mean a thing, but it was just crazy enough to be one of the best golf lessons I've ever had. It was crazy enough to remember.

I "sit down" slightly to let my knees bend a little, to make sure my legs are not locked like those of a folding bridge table. (You have to let the tension out of every muscle in your body, only keeping a comfortably firm grip on your club with the correct fingers.)

all clubs should lie flat for hitting — *not tilted up*

Then I size up the line to the hole. A lot of people just step up and slam at the ball in the general direction of the 20 acres ahead of them. You ought to want to stay within an alley 20 feet wide on your long shots. Wanting to and doing it are two different things.

I waggle the club head a little to renew my feeling of the weight of the club head. I once took a lesson from Ernest Jones and he drew from his pocket a knife on the end of a long piece of string, which he asked me to swing back and forth. "You can't push the knife with the string, can you?" he said. "The only way you can get the knife to move is to swing it." *That* is the feeling you must have in every golf swing you swing. A golf club is not a poker or a fly swatter. It is a weight on the end of a mere connecting shaft.

(Ernest Jones, by the way, is one of golf's great original and pioneer thinkers and philosophers. He has influenced a lot of teachers and influenced them right. You should have his book, *Swinging Into Golf* [Whittlesey House, New York] in your golf library.)

Then I get my feet wide enough apart to feel firm. They say about the width of your shoulders is right. But I know that I mustn't be too firm. One of my faults is that I sometimes stand there like an iron statue and try to hit the ball flatfooted. One day as I walked up to tee off a ball, one of my daughters shouted at me, "Be supple!" Well, *there* was another line or phrase just silly enough to stick in my mind.

I try to keep my weight more on my toes than on

The hands should not be out stiff like this

– nor sagged like this

Strike a comfortable, happy medium like this

my heels, because you sort of throw yourself with the follow-through, and you can't throw a lot of dead weight, which is what you have if you are set down, like a brick out-house, on your heels.

Then I set my head at a level and resolve to keep it there until I have hit the ball, but not too long, because you can lock yourself in a knot by over-protracted head fixation.

If you raise your head as you hit, you're raising the hub of the wheel which your golf swing is. You top the ball. If you lower your hub, you dig. You've got to think of keeping your head as still at the moment of contact as if you were getting your picture taken. In spite of this, I believe the head moves slightly from left to right. Remember, the one great thing to bear in mind about golf is that you can't play it with rigor mortis. I'm sure you can lock your head so tight that it locks your whole swing. The pros and the books all tell us to keep our heads still, knowing full well that we are going to move them a little, and knowing that if they told us to move them, we'd move them a mile. Ralph Guldahl puts it, "Be as stationary as possible."

I'd say, keep your head still, but relax it . . . and relax the neck muscles that go with it.

As you address the ball, be sure that the bottom of the club head is lying flat on the ground. And see that the club shaft goes straight down—that your hands are not ahead of the ball.

An excellent way to practice your swing is to stand with your back to the sun and watch your shadow to see how much your head moves—or doesn't.

After you've hit the ball, the story is different. If you stay with your head down, your arms can't go out toward the hole, and you pull them around under you to the left, and you draw the ball to the left.

As my first motion, I like to do a little forward press. This means a slight movement toward the hole with my body (except my head), mostly with my left leg and knee. This helps me to feel that I am going to work "under the level of my head," and it seems to unlock my legs, and also to warm up my motor a little.

Then I make up my mind that this is no difficult feat I am about to undertake, and that I don't need to be in any panic or in any hurry.

"When I can see your club go back, you get a good hit," said a wise old golfing friend of mine in Florida. I haven't any train to catch. The ball would still be there, even if I took five minutes. (My friend might not.)

Go back slowly enough to retain your poise, but not so slowly as to break your swing into a "go-up" and a "come-down."

I try to throw the club head back in a straight line just as far as I can—*just as far away from my body as possible*. But I don't advise *lifting* or poking it out there with a ramrod feeling in your left arm. Rodney Howard, at Vero Beach, told me to "throw it out" to the right, and that the throw would straighten my left arm and also take care of my pivot. But you can't do this with rubbery wrists, although this is where you start to feel the clubhead work. Eddie Loos once told a golfer in Pasadena that his swing was "too wristy at the start." Keep the hands and wrists firm; everything else relaxed.

If you lift the club head abruptly up from the ground with your hands, you'll surely get tack hammer results. Go back "as one piece" and let the back of your shoulders turn scornfully toward the hole.

Percy Boomer in his *On Learning Golf* (Alfred A. Knopf, New York), which is the most delightful and most intellectual golf book I've ever read, asks you to imagine that you are standing in a barrel. That means that you can't sway or duck. You can't do anything but pivot on a fixed level.

As you turn, uncramp your hips.

(I thought of calling this book *Golf Without Cramps*.)

The turn on the backswing will put you in hitting position, straighten your shot and lengthen your shot.

Let that left shoulder turn clear around on your upswing. Let the left hip turn one-half the way. Let the
left knee turn in. But, in spite of all this, don't let your
hands get around to the rear of you too far.

As you go back, your left knee turns toward your
right knee, but it does not dip or sag. The left foot
rises, so that you can keep the two knees about on the
same level. The right leg should be kept straight, but
not locked. Don't be a knee dipper.

Don't open your hands at the top of the swing and
let the club slop around.

Above everything else, don't overswing and lose
control of the club. You don't need a long backswing
to get distance. Craig Wood, one of the longest hitters
of all time, used only a three-quarter swing. He said:
"When you overswing, the club head power is spent
before you reach the ball, with the result that you
meet the ball out of control and get a hook, slice, or
a dubbed shot. If you reduce the arc of your swing,
you need less pivot, and greatly reduce the hazard of
losing control."

Then I try to linger slightly at the top of my backswing. Sometimes, up there, I catch myself saying to
myself, "There's no hurry about all this." I like to feel
a little lag at this point. I like to feel the clubhead particularly at this point. In an article in *Golfing Maga-*

too much
back swing
is bad

zine, which is one of the joys I get out of golf ($1 a year, published March through July, Chicago), Tommy Armour, speaking of the several things all good golfers do, once wrote, "They are all slow at the top of the swing." *That* is where timing is achieved. That is where you must feel music. That is where you start your beautiful, confident stroke at the ball, I hope.

If you are hurried and frantic at the top of your swing, you can't play good golf. This, more than anywhere else, I believe, is where the golfers are separated from the dubs.

Grantland Rice says that 80 per cent of all golfers never finish the backswing before the downswing is under way.

You can't properly start a downswing unless you have finished an upswing. Watch the flying trapeze artists in the circus for help with your swing.

The pros sometimes forget to tell us about that slight lag at the top—that "pause that refreshes." They have been swinging well so long that they have successfully blended their upswing and downswing, and they forget that we neophytes want to get up there and dash back quickly because the ball might go somewhere while we're away. Several years ago a pro said to me, "Your backswing is nice and slow, but take that quick chop out of your downswing."

this is how the hands
should look at the
top of the back swing

Rodney Howard, however, told me that if I got my backswing *too* slow, I'd unconsciously try to make up for lost time on the downswing.

Should you cock your wrists as you reach the top of your swing? Yes. But the pros say that you don't have to worry about this; that the weight of the club head will cock your wrists for you if you hold your wrists relaxed enough to let them cock. If you try cocking them too much, you may overswing. The club shaft should go no lower than horizontal.

Too much wrist cock will give you an undependable stroke.

Now all you've got to do is to hit the ball pretty, and *keep going with it*. Clarence McCarthy, one of the best of the old time teachers, told me that golf is played not on a course of 6,000 yards, but in a stretch of 6 inches—the tiny distance during which the club head is in contact with the ball. That's true, but what you do before you arrive at that short stretch, and what you do for several feet afterwards, somehow affects your behavior within the 6 inches. If you pinch in your arms after you've hit the ball, you were pinching them in as you hit the ball, because you'll surely get a sour hit.

Fling through and far out, and let your club head

Don't get the hands
ahead of the club head
as you hit, or you'll surely
get a slice. The best.
way to prevent this is
to wait a little at the
top of your back swing
to feel the "throw" of
the club head

draw you up into a long, graceful finish of your swing.
Let your arms flow out relaxed to the hole.

Keep *wide* on both sides.

The whole swing must be kept moderately slow,
and rhythmical. A lot of people and four pros told
me to slow down my backswing, but it was not until
I reached pro Number 5, that anybody told me to slow
down my *down*swing.

If you get yippy or yanky or hysterical at any point
of your swing, it will go haywire.

One of the best descriptions of a good swing that
I've ever read is Percy Boomer's: "Golf rhythm is a
delayed dragging feel of the club head, developed from
the power of the legs, kept under control by the braced
turning of the hips, and finally loosened into a free,
untrammeled movement of the arms outward and
around the left side." It will take me the rest of my
golfing life to digest *that. That's* what I like about golf.

I used to stay on my left foot and push my left
hip toward the hole on the upswing. You can't hit a
long ball without transferring your weight from one
foot to another. Even on approach shots I think you
have to feel this transfer. You have to feel golf in your
whole body.

I also used to fire and fall back. Pro Jerry Gian-
ferante told me I had "dissension" in my swing. The

You can't hit
from way over there;
keep your head
over the ball, and
swing under
your head

ball was going forward, and I was pulling backward. At impact I'd rare back, and sometimes even step back:

You can't get distance hitting a golf ball when you are backing away from it.

It's easy to see that you should be "feeling forward movement" all through the down swing, although you should be hitting against a firm left side for added power.

I suppose you know that long shots have to be hit from the inside out. It's paradoxical, but you have to hit outward and across the ball in order to get it to go straight.

It's good practice to walk away from the tee and take a few swings in the grass and see if the scars of your swing in the grass are from the inside out. If the scars turn in, practice until you get them to sweep out.

This, however, does not mean that you must develop a scythe-like swing, around your torso or hips. The arc of your swing must, on the other hand, be pretty upright.

Imagine a hoop standing up pretty straight. That's the upright swing, and it's right. If the hoop is tilted way back, that's a flat swing, and it's wrong.

So, when you pivot, don't get your hands away behind you as if you were swinging a baseball bat. Get them just slightly behind you, and up high.

"Firing and falling back"

VERY BAD

YOU CAN'T
HIT IF YOUR
CLUB HEAD
STARTS OUT HERE

LINE TO HOLE

CORRECT PATH OF SWING

YOU

One advantage of the upright arc is that it gives you more of a chance to hit the ball. With a low swing, you are with the line to the hole for only a fraction of an inch, like this:

But with an upright swing, you are going toward the hole for several inches, like this:

UPRIGHT SWING

LINE TO HOLE

An upright swing makes a natural hub of your head and shoulders.

However, it is possible to go back *too* upright. This may be one cause of slicing and digging into the turf.

Many duffers merely swivel their bodies around laterally. The good golf swing is more of a seesaw or teeterboard motion, with the left shoulder dipping low on the backswing, and the right shoulder (not the body) dipping low at impact—the head staying steady all the while.

If you stand too far away from the ball, it will give you too flat a swing, which may cause you to hook. Standing too close will cause you to slice and shank.

If you have a round stomach, you may have to learn how to get along with a flat swing.

As you swing through, don't pinch in. Look at the photos in the golf books and magazines and see how beautifully the good players let themselves go out toward the hole.

Me, I frequently hug my shots in, and cut across the ball and get a short shot or a fade. I'm an introvert at a time when I should be an extrovert. And I'm anxious to see how well I've hit my shot. I look something like this:

I PEEK UP
AND PINCH IN
—AND GET A SLICE

—WHEN I SHOULD KEEP MY DOME DOWN AND THROW OUT AFTER THE BALL WITH MY HANDS AND ARMS

Try a practice swing on each tee, to make sure you are full of "let-go."

Mike Kundrat says, "Stay with it longer."

No curly-me-cues at the end of your follow-through, either.

And, above all things, don't rare back off your left leg as you hit. A golf swing needs a base on that left leg, as you go through.

Someone once told me, "Let the club head pull you off your right foot and pull you through."

You sort of cast out to the hole, almost as if you were throwing the club away.

89

I've been told that most duffers lunge with their shoulders, instead of hitting with their hands. Fact is, you might almost say you should hit with the thumb and forefinger of your right hand, as that is where the feel of the club largely lies.

Jimmy Demaret says, "Hold the golf club as if it were a knife or fork."

As opposed to approach shots, which are hit, the long shots are *swept* away.

Of course, when you get up to swing, you can't possibly remember all the things that have to be remembered. But as time passes, you can reduce to a few points the most important things you simply have to remember, and as you walk up to take your shot and as you stand there, you had better remember them.

When driving off the tee, here are the things I try to remember to do:

1. get my head "level"—relax my arms and legs—"get supple";
2. sole the club flatly on the ground, and see that I do not grip it in such a way as to twist or tilt it;
3. do a slight forward press;
4. throw out to a very slow wide backswing along the ground;
5. let my shoulders turn;

6. wait for "the pause that refreshes" at the top;
7. fling out *toward the hole;* throw my arms away; let my head come up with the swing, after I have hit the ball;
8. avoid turning my hands over as I hit the ball; let the pull of the club turn them over later, nearer the top of the follow-through.

If I get fussed or hurried and muff one of these, I get a bad shot.

In playing a long shot from the fairway, place the ball a little farther back from your left toe than for a tee shot.

You've gotta be surer than ever to keep your head down until you've hit, so you'll get under the ball. You have no wooden tee to compensate for a half inch of carelessness in raising your skull.

Don't try to scoop or lift the ball with your hands. Smack it square in the derrière, and the loft of the club face will get the ball up. The worse the lie, the loftier the club you should use. In reality you spank the ball squarely with a wood, and hit down into it maliciously with an iron.

If you are troubled with slicing, hooking, and similar diseases, see the chapter on Traps and Other Troubles, later in the book.

91

finish with your belt buckle to the hole

CHAPTER 5

You've Gotta Take Aim

A LOT OF OUR GOLF SHOTS GO WRONG SIMPLY BE-
cause we aim 'em wrong.

Most of the time we just step up and swat the ball
in the general direction of the green and trust heaven
it will be one of our lucky shots.

"If the playing professionals contributed no more
thought to shot making than most of the gallery think,
they would starve to death in one season," said Ralph
Leaf, a good teaching pro. "There never has been and
never will be a man who can hit a ball carelessly and
break 90 consistently."

Golf requires a lot more thought than we think.

You have to think of yourself as a gun, and you have to set your sights and fix your range and trajectory just as carefully as if you were shooting at a duck.

Even in the longest shots, sight the line to the target, as you do in putting.

As you get near the green, figure the slope and the roll and the run, and decide on *the exact spot* on which you want the ball to land. A child knows a round object will roll downhill, but this fact doesn't seem to occur to many adult golfers.

Choose your club with as much care as if you were a surgeon choosing an instrument.

Make sure that your feet are set in the line of your aim. Many of the shots that go way off yonder do so simply because our toes are in a line to way off yonder.

Make sure that your hands are on the club in such a way as not to throw your shot off line.

Try a practice swing to rehearse the feel of your hands, the extent of your backswing and the power of your stroke. Feel the line on which your club face must go through the ball.

Look at the way your club face is set. Is it squarely at right angles to the line of flight? A lot of our bad shots are due merely to our angling the club face the wrong way. Figure how you want the paddle to be as it comes through the ball.

A golf ball is going to go only in the direction the club face goes.

Then press the trigger and fire.

You'll get a good shot if you let your swing go out beautifully along the line you have visualized in the manner you have imagined.

If you sprinkle your swing with alum, or lurch or lunge, or rare back or slump or yank up, you won't get a bull's eye any more than you would if you kicked a cannon at the moment of discharge.

Frank Stranahan says that Ben Hogan is a constant reminder to all the other top players not to be brainless or careless. He says that Ben doesn't do a thing without having determined that it represents good logic.

Logic? How many of us fair-to-middlers have ever thought of that word in connection with golf?

I talked to a teaching pro in Miami one day, and he told me of watching Bobby Jones in one of his tournaments. Bobby was playing badly until about the sixth hole; then his game improved miraculously. After the match, the pro asked Bobby what had happened. Bobby answered: "I simply started looking at the pin and deciding that that was where I wanted the ball to go."

Much bad golf is merely the result of ordinary bad marksmanship.

let golf
play you

CHAPTER 6

Let Golf Play You

I AM CONFIDENT THAT GOLF WOULD PLAY ITSELF
pretty well if we didn't interfere with it.

Almost every error we make is the result of our
putting the brakes on somewhere.

When a golf swing goes wrong, it is usually the
result of our locking some set of muscles. We tighten
up, hug in, hold back, cramp, and indulge in various
and sundry constrictive spasms which produce abortive
results.

If you pinch in on a putt instead of letting the
putter float out in a straight line toward the hole, the

ball will go to the left of the hole as sure as the Lord made little apples. And so on, up through every stroke of the game.

Every expert at any game, or at any art involving physical skill, has had to learn how to let go of muscles. They tell me it is very hard for pianists to learn how to let go of back muscles. I took hundreds of dancing lessons during one decade of my life and one of the hardest things I had to learn was to let go in the muscles in my shoulders. In golf, there are a dozen points at which you can lock your muscles and defeat your swing.

You can even look at the ball too hard, and lock a lot of muscles in the back of your neck which will spoil your swing.

You can lock arm muscles, back muscles, leg muscles, knee muscles and muscles all over your body— all to the detriment of your game.

Percy Boomer says that golf is a *passive* game— that its dominating sensation should be passivity. He says that the worse he feels, the better he plays. I've seen some mighty good golf out of guys with hangovers. They're too bushed to play too hard.

Percy Boomer says that all the good golf maxims of the ages enjoin passivity—"Take it easy," "Don't press," etc.

Tommy Armour, sitting at the lesson tee at Boca

Raton, said, "I want to set them the example of *educated languor*."

All my life I've been trying to learn cartooning, and one of the first things I learned about comic art was that if you want to draw funny you have to let go. I learned early in life that *the hardest thing on earth to control is abandon*.

To quote Chick Evans again: "One should hit the ball in a carefree way, but not carelessly."

The semantics of the game can sometimes add to its tension. For instance, "grip" is the wrong word for the action of holding a golf club. Harry Vardon speaks of the grip being sometimes improved by finger injuries, which enforce a lighter grip.

Golf lacks the "flow" of tennis and other sports. You have, in golf, the opportunity to stand there and work yourself up into a cataleptic state every time you swing at the ball.

Most of us can take a pretty swing at a dandelion. But a golf ball in front of us terrorizes us into a fine set of tensions.

Tension is the main cause, too, of hurry. We go back with a jerky backswing and zip down into a lightning-like downswing because we are tense. We try to play golf instead of letting golf play itself—instead of letting golf play *us*.

Without relaxation there can be no g[...]
you knew perfectly every paragraph of a [...]
on how to play perfect golf, you couldn't do it withou[...]
complete relaxation. Relaxation is the number one
requisite of a good golf swing.

At no point in your swing should there be any
evidence of jerk or sudden effort.

You are not in the stockyards killing a steer.

Smoothness adds to force, because it is momentum
and rhythm, not mauling, which gives power to your
swing.

Sammy Snead says that the force of a golf swing
is "gathered." You can't wham it from the top.

"Good golf is easy to play," says Ernest Jones,
"and easy golf is enjoyable golf." This man, Ernest
Jones, should be in every golfer's life to some extent.
As I've suggested before, get his book, and when and if
you go to New York and can arrange it, take a few
lessons from him, at Spalding's on Fifth Avenue.

He'll teach you that a golf club is not a club.
(Wrong semantics again.)

"Unless you can feel what you are doing with the
club head, you cannot possibly have any idea or sense
of timing."

Jones says you must feel the "pull" outward of the
club head, as you do in whirling a weight on a string.

99

After all, golf is more like playing with a yo-yo than ringing the bell with a sledgehammer at a county fair.

Even pivoting will take care of itself, if you let golf play you.

One serious point of possible tension is in the right knee on the downswing. Keep that knee stiff and you can't possibly let go out at the ball.

Sammy Snead says, "You must be more rubber than iron."

The Scots tell us to "play sloppy." (But, just the same, you have to be a little crisp about it.)

The habit some of us have of "firing and falling back" is nothing more or less than tension. As we hit the ball, we're opposing it with every muscle in our body. We finish on our right foot instead of our left. We constrict every limb. Common sense should tell us that if we respond to the pull of the club head it will take us naturally over onto the left foot.

Bobby Jones says that the three things that contribute most to tension are (1) a hard grip, (2) undue extension of the arms because we stand too far from the ball, (3) a too-wide separation of the feet. When we combine the three, we might as well be tied in chains.

Bobby says the chief center of relaxation is the knees.

Golf is easy. We just make it hard by getting all ossified when we swing.

Let golf play you.

HEROLD AT 92

"I'm going to master this game if it takes me the rest of my life"

CHAPTER 7

"I'm Too Old To Learn— I'll Never Play Any Better"

ONCE IN A WHILE I HEAR SOMEBODY SAY, "I'M TOO old to learn—I'll never play any better." I darn near cross him off my list, then and there. While a certain amount of resignation is at times necessary for the enjoyment of golf, there should always be a little fight left in us at any age, and I believe the thing that gives me real zest for golf is my undying desire to learn to play a better game, and my firm belief that I shall.

And when I'm too old to play, I'm going to get a kick out of sitting on the sidelines, and talking about the game. (I remember when the most ardent polo fan on the Pacific Coast and one of its greatest financial backers was a blind man. He was on the sidelines at every game in Los Angeles.)

One of my middle-aged golf acquaintances in Florida was a man to whom, for some reason, I had taken a mild dislike. I didn't know him very well, had never played golf with him. Just didn't think I'd like him. But one day I was thrown into a game with him and he made a remark which completely changed my feelings toward him. He was not a very good golfer, and he had just hit a poor shot. "I'm going to learn this game if it takes me the rest of my life," he said. In an instant he had my respect and esteem, and I've liked him ever since.

I met another fellow down there early one season, who was playing terrible golf. He had been an excellent golfer in his time, but he had had an accident and had cut one arm badly above the wrist, and was having to learn the game all over again without some of the muscles in that arm. His attempt at a long swing was something to behold, because he had to compensate for the things he couldn't do with his bad arm. He hit all of his approach shots with his one good arm. I think he was scoring at the rate of about 120 the first few times I played with him.

"I'm going to stay here until I break 80, or until they bury me on the first fairway," he said.

He practiced every morning, and was sometimes so discouraged that he almost cried. And he played every afternoon. He was a golf maniac if I ever saw one.

But he made rapid improvement, and in a little over two months he pulled up in front of our house and came in and said that he was starting home to Illinois.

"Did you break 80?" I asked.

"Yes, I got a 73 yesterday."

In a book called *Outwitting Your Years* by Clarence William Lieb, M.D. (Prentice-Hall, New York), I have just read the following: "Agephobia is an entity of fearful mien. But it is a wholly unnecessary affliction and it can be self-cured by anyone who has the strength of character and good common sense to realize that it is not chronological age but biological age, and, to an even greater degree, spiritual age that determine the health and happiness that are to be our lot in the later years of life."

Over General MacArthur's desk in Tokyo hung these words: "Youth is not a time of life—it is a state of mind. . . . You are as young as your faith, as old as your doubt; as young as your self confidence, as old as your fear; as young as your hope, as old as your despair." Tack this up in your gallery of golf mottoes.

The most inspiring story I know in golf annals is the story of Mark G. Harris.

Mark Harris took up golf at 65, broke 90 at 67, was shooting in the 70's at 69, became the foremost authority in the country on approaching and putting, and wrote the best book I've ever read on putting and chip shots. (See Chapter 2.) He even made a movie short for Paramount on chipping and putting.

D. Scott Chisholm watched Mark Harris one afternoon and reports: "He holes one out of three mashie shots at 35 feet and puts the other two within a foot of the hole. He holes one out of three mashie chips from 45 feet and puts the other two within 14 inches. He sinks three putts in succession at eight feet and repeats the feat at 14 feet. He sticks a golf tee in the ground at seven feet and hits it three times in succession." At age 69!

Many of the big golf pros have gone to Mark Harris to brush up on their short game and putting.

He developed his own system for putting, and it comes as near to being fool proof and jitter proof as any method you can adopt.

Mark Harris quotes a tough little gunman as saying, "A six-shooter makes all men equal," and adds that it's about the same with a putter. He says a putter equalizes the advantages gained by long drivers.

P. A. Velie wrote: "Mr. Harris, by the most persevering and assiduous practice, has made himself into such a skilled player of the short game that I am sure the results he achieved, in such a remarkably short time, are worthy of permanent record in the bibliography of golf for they must go far to smother the pernicious nonsense written and taught about the impossibility of learning the art of putting." Also, wrote Mr. Velie: "Every golfer should realize that when he misses a two-foot putt, he offsets his 250 yard drive in one single stroke." *

One of my best friends in Florida was Frank Wilson, at Vero Beach. Frank was the most passionate golf student I have ever known. I'm sure that his interest in golf kept him alive for many years. He was an invalid for many of the last years of his life, yet he was out on the course almost every day, hitting a few balls, giving free lessons, talking golf, or playing nine holes if he felt up to it. He spent the last three years of his life in bed, yet his interest in golf remained as intense as ever. His friends would drop in to see him for amusement

* Quoted in *Putting,* by Mark Harris (Reilly & Lee, Chicago).

and advice. "I'm having trouble with my No. 8 iron," they'd say, and Frank would straighten them out right there in his bedroom, practically on his deathbed. He knew more about what was going on on the golf course than many of us who were out on the course every day. He had had many friends among the world's top golfers in his time and could talk for hours about them and their methods.

Golf is a lovely thing when it can make a man as happy as that, under such adverse circumstances!

We put up a memorial drinking fountain for Frank Wilson near the fourteenth green at Vero Beach.

Jolly Foursome

CHAPTER 8

Don't Be So Damned Dull

A LOT OF GOLFERS ARE DAMNED DULL FELLOWS.

They whack the ball and then clop, clop, clop, clump, clump, clump down the fairway with little or nothing to say, and then hit the ball again, and clop, clop, clop.

Conversation, if any, is largely confined to comments on shots, and these are usually according to pattern.

Golf's not *that* serious.

For gawd's sake, try to be somewhat blithe about it as you go along. I like some irrelevant conversation with my golf, or some new kind of conversation about the old golf.

There is nothing more boresome than the conscientious blow-by-blow describer of his own game. "My drive went behind a tree on the left, and all I could do was to hit a short shot out onto the fairway. I took my 9 iron, but I hit a rock and went to the right and hit another tree, and it took me two to get out of the woods, and then I found myself in a bad lie on the fairway, etc., etc., etc."

Who cares?

There are a few of these blow-by-blowers in every club.

Then there are the over-dependable cliché boys who can be counted on for crack number 26, if circumstances call for it.

"That won't do you any harm."

"There isn't any hole there," if three of you have missed your putts.

"That's what comes of clean living."

"He went to church this morning."

"He ate his Wheaties."

"That's my partner!"

"You'll like that!"

"One!" if your opponent accidentally knocks his ball off his wooden tee.

"A rainmaker!"

"On the beach!"

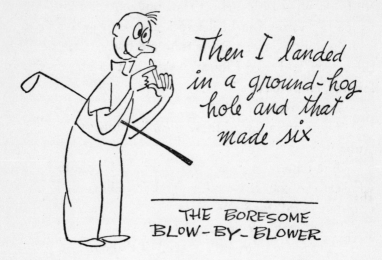

Then I landed
in a ground-hog
hole and that
made six

THE BORESOME
BLOW-BY-BLOWER

"You wuz robbed!"

Just a little mental effort would improve these or at least produce refreshing silence.

I'd almost rather play no golf than grim, plodding, mechanical, merely stick-to-the-subject golf.

Golf is not sacred, and there's no use getting so gosh-darned solemn about it.

At our little family golf course in Connecticut, we have tournaments ending on Labor Day, and, toward the end, the atmosphere gets almost sanctified. There aren't more than a handful of really good golfers in the club, yet the whole club goes golf righteous. You could hear a pin drop on the first tee, and I have suggested that we get a pipe organ for that tee, and an organist from one of the local churches to play sacred music. Perhaps also a parson to start each day off with prayer.

The interest is not primarily in golf; it's largely social. People who haven't taken the trouble to practice a putt or an approach shot or take a lesson all summer are taking golf with grim solemnity.

Before the tournaments are over, the community has often had a few fights, and there are great hopes that one of the community stinkers will get his or her pants whipped off by a more likeable character.

In my mind, this is all a desecration of golf.

It's making a cat-and-dog fight out of a game

which we all should be trying sincerely to learn to play better.

If we were tournament pros and our bread and butter depended on golf, we perhaps might be justified in concentrating fiercely on our game, to the exclusion of lightness, laughter, nature and the amenities.

But even some of the pros have played white hot golf without losing their, if any, senses of humor.

The more I read of golfers, past and present, the more I feel that swashbuckling Walter Hagen was the outstandingly picturesque character of them all —the top philosopher and the greatest funster of the lot—and no mean golfer, to boot.

Percy Boomer says that Hagen was not only one of the greatest golfers, but was one of the most buoyant. (There's the word I have been wanting!) "Whenever he played he simply oozed with the joy of life. The more he was up against it the better he played.

"Please note that the Hage did *not* concentrate in the accepted sense. He did not shut extraneous matters out of his mind; he merely shut them out of his golf. While he was playing he would talk intelligently about any subject that cropped up, stocks and shares, eating and drinking, politics or puritanism. Nothing, neither wind nor weather, bad greens, tight corners, or unduly chatty opponents, ever made the Hage tense. Consequently golf never exhausted him; he was as fresh at the end of a championship as he was at its beginning." (This is from *On Learning Golf*, and I urge you again to buy a copy.)

Perhaps the most delightful golfing companion I ever had was Earl Derr Biggers, author of the Charlie Chan stories. (This was in a previous, early spurt of golf in which I indulged years ago, only to drop the game for many years before really going loco about it.)

One day when Earl and I were playing in Pasadena, he hit a bit of grass into the air and seriously put it back in place.

"A very ethereal divot, Earl," I said.

"Just a sprig of mignonette," he replied.

"How do you hit 'em so far?" somebody asked Babe Zaharias.

"I just loosen my girdle and let the ball have it."

Jim Turnesa says none of us will ever shoot the perfect golf game—eighteen holes-in-one. So why take it so seriously?

And remember what Ring Lardner said: "If you hit a ball with a mashie it will sometimes go farther than if you miss it with a driver."

Don't be a gratuitous "lesson giver." Just keep your large mouth shut about what you see wrong with the other fellow's golf. You might help him, but he'll

like it better if you don't. Personally, I like a suggestion now and then from a better golfer. I like to be told
if I'm lifting my head or teeing the ball too high or
yielding persistently to some other bad habit. But I
don't want a running discussion of my golfing faults
. . . that is, from anybody other than the pro.

Above everything, don't try to teach golf to anybody in your own family. We golf nuts are usually
anxious to have all members of our family develop into
good golfers. There's no better way to kill the instinct
of golf in wives or in sons or in daughters than to give
'em a free lesson with every stroke. One of my daughters
showed a lot of golf promise, but I killed golf for her by
telling her too much and urging her too hard. I've had
a few fights with my wife because I wouldn't let her go
on hitting them lousily. Don't get serious with your
family on the golf course. Leave them at home, let
them play with somebody else, or keep still. Golf in-
struction from the pro is not too expensive; better let
him be the doctor when it comes to members of your
family. When you go out for golf with the family, make
it fun.

I played with a man and his wife and their daughter the other day. The parents were eager to have the
girl get interested in golf, yet the father criticized almost every shot, and the mother annoyed her almost

as much by overpraising shots that the girl knew were only fair. I could see that they were making a golf hater out of her. The whole thing would have been better if it had been kept on a straight kidding basis.

But don't practice until you are purple

CHAPTER 9

Good Golf Is Shaken
Only Out of a Practice Bag

I'VE SAID THAT GOLF WILL PLAY ITSELF. BUT YOU must co-operate.

I don't think you can get the most fun out of golf unless you are willing to practice.

You can learn to enjoy practice almost as much as you enjoy playing. It's a pleasure to feel yourself finding the knack of hitting a ball with a certain club from a certain spot to a certain spot.

Babe Zaharias says: "Practice should be approached as just about the most pleasant recreation ever devised, besides being a necessary part of golf."

And after you learn golf, you forget it and you have to go out and re-learn it. Discovery and loss and re-discovery—that's golf. But the re-learning comes more easily than the learning.

We don't hope to get as good as Ben Hogan, but if he, with his ability, still has to practice a lot, we ought to be able to practice a little. Ben says that if you want to develop a good swing, you have to hit thousands upon thousands of shots in succession, day after day, year after year.

Well, then, either practice or learn to take it philosophically if you play poorly.

I think a practice bag is one of the first things a golfer should buy, yet I daresay not one golfer in a hundred owns one. But not one golfer in a hundred gets the fun out of golf of which he is capable. Combine the fun of playing with the fun of *learning*—that's my theme song in this book.

But don't practice bad shots over and over. Your practice sessions should be interspersed with an occasional lesson, so that you will know what you're practicing. No point to practicing mistakes. Get somebody to watch you who knows, and make sure you just aren't making a bigger fool out of yourself.

You don't have to knock yourself out with your practice sessions.

Scientific tests prove that the best way to learn anything is to practice for short periods, with intervals between the periods. You thus not only eliminate fatigue and boredom, you allow time for maturation of the nerve connections which have been exercised.

As William S. Knudsen said, "It still takes nine months to have a baby."

William A. Rossi says that though you can rush the act of learning, you cannot rush the *absorption* of learning; the brain has what might be termed a learning saturation rate. This can even be proved with mice in a maze. In a now well-known test, mouse number 1 was given five trials a day and found the exit after forty trials. Mouse number 5 was given one trial every third day and found the exit after only thirteen trials.

It's all right for Ben Hogan to get his hands blood raw from practice, but the top golfer who has a practice philosophy perhaps more fitting for us less serious golfers is Bobby Locke. Bobby doesn't believe in knocking himself cold with practice. Before a tournament round he hits only a few shots with each club, then spends 10 to 15 minutes getting the feel of his putter. He practices only until he has regained his confidence with each club. He doesn't believe in hitting away until he's lost his confidence again and has to regain it.

But it's logical that we tired business men and

exhausted mammas and bridge players need some kind of warming up. Most of us males have been using only our desk muscles and fanny muscles most of the week.

There's some merit in the suggestion that all golf courses should be 19 holes—with the first one not counting.

That's why I think mulligans are all right on the first tee. Most of us players come right out from bending over a hot desk or changing a hot diaper. We're entitled to a short period of readjustment to the new life outdoors.

One thing to remember when practicing is to hit every practice shot as if it counted. Don't wham away at a lot of balls in rapid succession, just to empty the bag. Be just as thoughtful and deliberate in practice as you're supposed to be when playing.

Gene Sarazen suggests we concentrate our practice on the one club with which we were playing most poorly on the preceding round.

I agree with Gene when he says also that every course should provide practice traps. You can't go out to a regular green on the course and slop a wheelbarrow load of sand onto it.

How are we duffers going to learn to feel cozy in a sand trap?

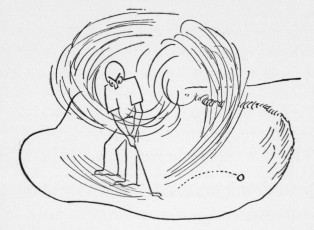

CHAPTER 10

Traps and Other Troubles

THE BEST GOLFERS ALIVE GET INTO TROUBLE NOW and then.

Those who stay alive are those who don't let these troubles get their blood pressures up.

A few years ago Dr. Frederic Brush, then 73, who with his son had won three Westchester father-and-son titles, made the amusing experiment of actually having his blood pressure tested in a sand trap. He muffed two shots and was pretty sore, and he had a medical colleague attach the pressure gauge manometer to his arm and found that his blood pressure had kited up 30 points.

The pros all say that a shot out of a trap is one of the easiest shots in golf. We ordinary mortal golfers are apt to dread it so pathologically that we may go practically into convulsions at the sight of the ball in the sand, and doom ourselves to several hacks in increasingly maddening succession.

I think the best thing to do is to get your pro to go out with you once in a while for a straight "trouble lesson." Take him to spots on the course in which you have actually had disaster—that deep trap on the 16th, that tall grass on the rear of the 6th, that rough to the right of the 5th, that side hill lie which you usually get on the 7th. There are tricks for getting out of all these troubles, and they are duck soup for your pro. He can take the nightmare out of them for you.

Traps

There are two kinds of shots out of sand: (1) a skim; (2) a blast.

Skim shot out of traps

The skim shot or clean shot is really the more difficult and dangerous of the two. The pros advise against trying it, but they admit there are times when it is all right. If the trap is shallow, the bank low, the lie clean, and the sand hard (as after a rain), you are perfectly justified in skimming the ball out.

With the skim shot, you hit the ball first and take a slight scoop of sand second. The ball is therefore placed back nearer a point in line with your right foot. The stance is more closed than for the blast shot.

You keep your head steady and you hit the ball with straight, firm arms. This, because the margin for "up and down error" is small.

For the same reason, don't bend your knees.

Go back slowly, to aid your accuracy.

When you come down, go straight out to the pin with the stiff left arm—not a wrist flip.

And may heaven grant that you don't go 20 yards over the green.

Use an 8 or 9 iron for this shot.

"Blasting" out of trap

In the first place, the blast isn't a blast shot at all. I used to rupture myself trying to "blast." The word is all wrong.

This shot is more a slap or a flip. But it isn't a stingy one.

The shape of the swing is actually much closer to a "U" than the shape of any other swing in golf.

This means that there is much easier wrist action

in it than in other shots. You pick the club head up pretty straight from the ball, instead of pushing it back along the sand.

Start this shot by squirming your feet down into the sand until you feel rock bottom.

The stance is open. That is, the left foot is way back from the line of flight.

The object is to take a pint or a quart of sand before you hit the ball. So you place the ball up forward in a line off your left toe. You lay the face of the club back until the rear of the club head is almost touching the sand. Stand close enough to the ball to insure digging. (It's illegal to touch the sand with your club before you hit it.)

Don't look at the ball. Look at the spot 1, 2 or 3 inches behind the ball where you want to hit. For shorter shots you hit 3 or even 4 inches back. For longer shots you hit closer to the ball. Dick Chapman says he tries to imagine that the ball has legs, and he deliberately tries to cut the legs from under it.

You've got to keep your head down more religiously than for any other golf shot, and it's harder to do because you're hysterically anxious to see what's going to happen. Let somebody tell you what has happened. Eventually you can look, but not now.

If you lift the noggin, you'll skim the shot, and

your ball will go way over the green, into the trap on the other side, and manic depression will set in and you'll crisscross the green several times and wind up with a 9. Later you'll have intestinal gas.

The back stroke for this shot is about the only one in ordinary golf which should go outside the line of flight. In other words, you hit from the outside in, and cut across the ball as you hit.

When you hit, hit down into the sand as far as you can.

And now we come to the most common mistake you can make in the blast shot, and that is the mistake of *not following through with the swing*. Nine times out of nine, the beginner hits into the sand and practically stops there, chicken-heartedly. You can cut down the power of your swing, but you must not cut down the distance of your follow-through. You simply have to let go out to the pin, even if it's only 15 feet away. Imagine a line for this follow-through.

Make sure your knees are relaxed for this shot.

Use a blaster or sand wedge or No. 11 iron.

Have your grip down on the club shaft.

If the sand is wet and heavy and you have to blast, put more power into your swing than you do in dry sand.

Aim to the left of the pin.

Rough going

In the rough near the green, use a No. 8 or 9 or a pitching wedge and use it like a knife. Lay the club face back. Open the stance. Swing up right, with a "U" shaped swing; this will help keep the long grass from wrapping itself around the club head. Don't stop your swing dead in the grass, but go up and out to the pin.

If you're in the deep rough far from the pin, don't try the impossible. Be satisfied to get out of your trouble without aspiring to great distance. As in other moments in golf, it's better to tackle one achievement at a time—not two.

When the winds do blow

We hamateurs pay lots less attention to the wind than the pros do. It's more important than you think. I've seen my score go up several points on windy days.

Wind is hard not only on our shots but hard on our nerves.

We must learn either to combat wind intelligently, or to cultivate a philosophical windy day acceptance of higher scores.

Wind coming at us head on calls for clubs with less loft and for swings that give us lower trajectories. On the tee, play the ball back farther toward the right foot, rather than tee it low.

In a brisk head wind, use a "punch shot," gripping the club low and hitting down on the ball. Both arms are firm and extended, and the hands are used for speed.

If the wind is coming from the right, aim farther to the right; if from the left, aim farther to the left. Even these shots should be kept as low as possible.

If the wind is coming from behind you, tee the ball higher than usual and play it higher than usual, to get the free ride that the wind will give it.

Lost in the woods

When your ball is under a tree, you have to play it flat. Stand so that the ball is off the right toe. Use a club with less loft and swing wide but not high. Don't get frantic and spoil your shot by trying to hit it too hard.

If you have to go over a tree that is fairly near you, play the ball off the left toe, lay the club face back, and swing full, with a pause at the top of the backswing and a graceful throw to the pin.

Hillside lies

On all hillside lies, the big fundamental idea is to follow the contour of the ground with your club head, and to adjust your stance to take care of the slope.

On downhill and uphill lies, you must place the ball where the lowest part of the swing will be. Says Ben Hogan in *Power Golf:* "Think of the relation of the ball to the arc of the swing rather than of whether to play it off one foot or the other."

Downhill. Play the ball farther back if the slope is steep. Flex the right leg. The weight is more on the left. Iron clubs are best, because they help lift. You need a club with loft to get the ball up.

The back swing is more upright than usual because that, too, helps to lift the ball.

You should play to the left, because the ball is inclined to slice to the right.

Keep the club head going on down hill, following as close to the ground as possible.

Uphill. Stand a little closer to the ball and play the ball halfway between your feet.

Keep the weight of the body more on the right foot, and flex the left knee.

Swing flatter than for a downhill lie. Keep the club head low on the backswing, and follow the contour of the slope with your club head.

Aim to the right to avoid the tendency to hook this kind of shot.

Let the club travel up, following the slope of the hill.

On uphill lies you need a club with less loft to get the ball up, because you are already hitting the ball up.

Sidehill, ball above feet. Shorten your grip on the club, or play it farther away from the feet. The point is to give yourself room enough to swing. Swing flat. Take a slow backswing. The tendency is to pull to the left, so aim to the right. Line the feet up slightly to the right. Keep your weight slightly forward and your hands low.

You can't get so much power into a swing in this position, so use a longer club than you would for the same distance on flat ground.

You'll tend to hit the ball off the toe of the club. To counteract this, address it off the heel of the club.

Sidehill lie, ball below feet. Hands low like this:

Be sure to keep your head and body down. The tendency is to slice, so aim to the left. Line the feet up slightly to the left.

The danger in this shot is that of topping the ball, so use a longer club than usual. Don't pivot as much as on flat ground.

To cure a slice

We slice because we hit from the outside in. This brings the club face across the ball in such a way as to put a clockwise spin on it, which means that it ends up in Mrs. Wiggs' cabbage patch to the right of the fairway.

Here are some suggestions for curing slices:

1. Hit from in to out. Make your target slightly to the right so you won't cut across the ball.
2. Get the right hand down under the club shaft more—but not too far or you will hook.
3. Close the stance if it's too open. (That means get your left foot back and your right foot forward more.)
4. Tighten the finger grip on your left hand.
5. Be sure you let yourself pivot on the upswing. This will help you hit from in to out.
6. Be sure you don't hit with your hands ahead of the ball. Wait at the top, and feel that club

head and fling it so that it beats your hands to the hit.

7. Keep control of your club at the top so that you won't flop it down from the outside in.

8. Keep your left arm firm.

9. Swing through all the way; don't quit at the ball.

One *sure way* to slice is to aim to the left to get away from the woods or rough on the right into which you have been habitually slicing. This almost guarantees that you'll hit from outside in, and give the ball that accursed clockwise spin.

Shanking, which is a malignant form of slicing, is usually caused by collapsing the left arm, so that you are pointing your left elbow at the hole as you hit. This turns the club face at a 45 degree angle to the line of flight, and you get one of the most depressing results in this glorious game of golf. Another thing that will do it is too early a turn of the body to the left.

If you *want* to slice, open the stance more, hit somewhat from the outside in, and get your hands over to the left more on top of the club.

To cure a hook

A hook is a shot that goes away over into the cemetery to the left, because the club face is drawn across the ball from the inside out, giving it counter-clockwise spin.

Here are some possible cures:

1. Try opening the stance.
2. Be sure that the club face is not toed in to the left at the start of the swing.
3. Don't get the right hand too far over to the right—under the shaft.
4. Don't let the right elbow get too far away from the body on the downswing.
5. Be sure you don't turn your hands over as you hit the ball.
6. Don't lunge.

Pulling is something like hooking, except that a pulled ball *goes* to the right, while a hooked ball *whirls* to the right because of the spin you have put on it.

If you *want* to hook, close your stance, and get your right hand under the club more.

How to cure sclaffing

Sclaffing is a common malady among 90 shooters. It consists in hitting behind the ball.

This comes largely from curtseying with knee dips in the swing both ways, and from starting to throw the club head from the top of the downswing. The sclaffer usually throws his weight back onto his right foot as

132

he hits the ball, instead of "stepping into the shot" by shifting his weight to his left foot. The bad distribution of balance is usually accompanied by a duck of the right shoulder, and, wham, he hits the ground behind the ball.

How to cure skying

Skying is caused by (1) teeing the ball too high, (2) using a club with too shallow a face, (3) lifting the club up too abruptly on the backswing instead of pushing it far out with an extended left arm. Number three is usually followed by bringing the club and the weight down sharply. If you do this, you probably pop the ball upwards, and, as the wagsters say, you bring rain, and get white marks on top of your club head. Sometimes with this type of stroke you come right down on top of the ball and get the very opposite of skying—you drive the ball almost into the ground or along the ground.

A well hit long shot comes from a club head that has been traveling parallel with the ground for 6 inches —not for from 2 to 3 inches.

One other thing that can cause skying is turning the club head over at moment of impact. This results from rolling the wrists, or from getting too much right hand in the downswing.

"I haven't had a good shot all day until this one"

CHAPTER 11

Along About Here

ALONG ABOUT HERE, YOU ARE PROBABLY SAYING, "The hell with it!"

Well, just let the whole thing drop.

I agree with you that this is an awful lot of golf talk for one session. It's an awful lot of golf philosophy to absorb or refute at one or two sittings.

I'm assuming that you have read this book in one eager gulp and haven't skipped to the end to see how it comes out.

You could spend a week on many a single page of this book, maybe out in a sand trap with the book in one hand and a blaster in the other. And then the page wouldn't do you any real good unless you re-wrote it yourself.

Some of the best ideas I've had on golf have been some I've thought up myself while the pro was talking about something else.

After all, as I may have said before in this book, a man's golf is, in final analysis, between himself and his maker.

You don't have to take golf too seriously. But I'd like to be sure I've made the paradoxical point in this book that the more seriously you take it the more fun it is, and the less seriously, therefore, you have to take it.

The other day I played one of my best games, and I'll tell you why. The why was silly. I happened to be playing with a little grandmother at our Connecticut club—one of the best women players we have. Her swing was so soft and graceful that I caught relaxation from her. She couldn't swing powerful, so she swang easy and right.

Crazy things like that will help your golf tremendously.

"Next to the idiotic, the dull unimaginative mind

is the best for golf," wrote one of the old timers, Sir Walter Simpson.

But in commenting on this statement in *How To Play Golf* (Prentice-Hall, New York), Ben Thomson says: "I would qualify that by saying that the *outward appearance* of a dull, unimaginative mind is well suited for golf." And he adds that *inwardly* the successful golfer must be pretty alert.

What is a successful golfer?

I think it is the golfer who milks the game for every ounce of fun that it will give him, regardless of his score. But part of the fun is learning how to score better.

And a lot of the fun is in wanting like the dickens to learn how to play better, without letting it get you down if you don't.

And even when your golf is no good, you can say that it's better than walking down Sixth Avenue.

There have been days when all that I've got out of golf was the oxygen.

And no matter how bad the golf is, there's always that good, hot bath or that long drink to which to look forward, afterward . . . or both.

don herold
—
HERE LIES
A GOLFER;
DON'T
THEY ALL?